RICHARD STEARNS

LE▲D
LIKE IT
M▲TTERS
TO
G⊕D

STUDY GUIDE

EIGHT SESSIONS ON BECOMING
A VALUES-DRIVEN LEADER

An imprint of InterVarsity Press
Downers Grove, Illinois

InterVarsity Press
P.O. Box 1400, Downers Grove, IL 60515-1426
ivpress.com
email@ivpress.com

InterVarsity Press® is the book-publishing division of InterVarsity Christian Fellowship/USA®, a movement of students and faculty active on campus at hundreds of universities, colleges, and schools of nursing in the United States of America, and a member movement of the International Fellowship of Evangelical Students. For information about local and regional activities, visit intervarsity.org.

All Scripture quotations, unless otherwise indicated, are taken from The Holy Bible, New International Version®, NIV®. Copyright © 1973, 1978, 1984, 2011 by Biblica, Inc.™ Used by permission of Zondervan. All rights reserved worldwide. www.zondervan.com. The "NIV" and "New International Version" are trademarks registered in the United States Patent and Trademark Office by Biblica, Inc.™

While any stories in this book are true, some names and identifying information may have been changed to protect the privacy of individuals.

The publisher cannot verify the accuracy or functionality of website URLs used in this book beyond the date of publication.

Cover design and image composite: David Fassett
Interior design: Jeanna Wiggins
Image: compass illustration: © Sigit Mulyo Utomo / iStock / Getty Images Plus

ISBN 978-0-8308-4719-8(print)
ISBN 978-0-8308-4720-4 (digital)

Printed in the United States of America ∞

InterVarsity Press is committed to ecological stewardship and to the conservation of natural resources in all our operations. This book was printed using sustainably sourced paper.

P	22	21	20	19	18	17	16	15	14	13	12	11	10	9	8	7	6	5	4	3	2	1
Y	39	38	37	36	35	34	33	32	31	30	29	28	27	26	25	24	23	22	21

CONTENTS

INTRODUCTION

WELCOME! I'M GLAD YOU'VE JOINED ME on this journey toward thinking more about what it means to be a godly leader—whether in your chosen profession, at your church, at your school, in your neighborhood, or in your family—and then becoming one. Because good leaders can change the world in remarkable ways.

Leaders provide direction and vision, enabling groups to accomplish something that individuals alone could not have achieved. Think about any winning sports team or successful company. Why are they winning and accomplishing more? Leadership.

Leadership is the one critical ingredient that changes the world. Yet as Christian leaders, our first duty is faithfulness to God; it's the quality of our character and witness wherever we work. Successful outcomes are important too, but they shouldn't become our all-consuming goal.

As Christian leaders, our true purpose is to become part of Jesus' revolution to change the world, to help bring about a new relationship between God and humankind—a relationship that reconciles, restores, and heals the brokenness of the human race and renews God's creation, conforming it more to the character and likeness of God. Our part in that revolution begins where we work and live. And so God is looking for leaders "after his own heart," winsome leaders who will submit to his leading and trust him for the outcomes. A leader's character, values, and motives matter to God. While we value the "what" of our work, God values the "why" and the "how." We reward success, but God's bottom line is faithfulness.

This is why our leadership matters so much to God. Christian leaders are called to be change agents for Christ, bringing healing and restoration into the brokenness of their communities and workplaces. Good and godly leadership contributes to human flourishing when it creates cultures and environments that are fair, just, and caring. Christian leaders shape and influence institutions, and that matters. Integrity, excellence, humility, forgiveness, encouragement, trust, and courage are values of the kingdom of God. And when leaders incarnate those values, the world changes.

Second Corinthians 5:20 captures our role as Christian leaders: "We are therefore Christ's ambassadors, as though God were making his appeal through us." Ambassadors are called to embody the values, ideals, and character of the one they represent. It doesn't matter whether you consider yourself a leader or not. You're Christ's ambassador, his change agent. God has been present in your life since before you drew your first breath, and he wants to use all your talents, abilities, and life experiences to shape you and prepare you to serve his purposes.

I am not arguing that we don't strive for success as leaders. Success isn't a bad thing, it's just not the main thing. Character and competence are both honoring to God. When we focus first on being faithful to God in our lives and when our work is driven by the values of God's kingdom, he may very well bless us with successful outcomes. But qualities like integrity, humility, excellence, perseverance, generosity, courage, and forgiveness matter more to God than the most impressive resume of accomplishments. That's why I wrote *Lead Like It Matters to God*—to call Christian leaders to embrace and lead with those values.

The beauty of becoming a values-driven leader is that embracing positive values does not require us to master any exceptional new skills or techniques. Values-driven leadership is more about character than capabilities, more about being than doing, more about pleasing God than people. So I organized the book around seventeen values and leadership qualities that I believe are essential for a Christian leader to embody: surrender, sacrifice, trust, love, excellence, humility, integrity, vision, courage, generosity, perseverance, forgiveness, self-awareness, balance, humor, encouragement, and listening.

Throughout this guide, we're going to unpack each of these character qualities so we can learn the main lessons and develop and mature those values and traits in our lives and in our leadership so we can aspire to a different kind of success—the kind that truly matters to God.

The following eight sessions include all seventeen character traits I discuss in *Lead Like It Matters to God*, but for the sake of time, I've combined two to three characteristics in each session. You can go through each lesson individually or in a group. These lessons are designed to help you reflect honestly and vulnerably on how you're doing with these traits in your life and your leadership. But it doesn't end there. You must put them into practice!

To help you do that, I've broken each lesson into several parts: review, reflect, and practice. First, we'll review the key principle and Scripture passage for the value or trait we're studying, as well as some of the corresponding chapter material.

Second, we'll reflect on how that trait or value is most relevant to your experience and leadership setting. We talked about how important the "why" and "how" of leadership is to God; this is the place to ponder those aspects more deeply. Use these thoughts to prompt your self-evaluation—both individually and as a group—to move you into applying the key lessons to your own leadership.

Third, at the end of each chapter we'll give you practical ideas for putting these qualities into action right away. As you already know, the act of leadership is just that—acting, engaging, practicing. It is anything but static.

Leadership is important. It affects every dimension of our human experience. It can unite us, lift us, and inspire us to achieve great things. And good, values-based leadership provides us with that North Star of character that is so crucial to accomplishing God's purposes in our world.

SURRENDER, SACRIFICE, AND TRUST

VALUE 1: SURRENDER

Read chapter three of *Lead Like It Matters to God.*

Key Leadership Principle: The starting point of Christian leadership is total surrender.

Key Scripture: "Whoever wants to save their life will lose it, but whoever loses their life for me will find it." (Matthew 16:25)

For the Christian leader, we must start with surrender. In fact, the act of becoming a Christian begins with total surrender. God wants us to let go of everything we hold dear and lay those things at his feet for his service. Only then are we truly useful to God. He doesn't accept a compartmentalized life in which our careers are held back and kept outside our total submission to his purposes.

And God is not interested in bargaining, compromising, or negotiating our terms of surrender. He wants all of us. In the words of Oswald Chambers in *My Utmost for His Highest*: "If you have only come as far as asking God for things, you have never come to the point of understanding the least bit of what surrender really means. You have become a Christian based on your own terms."

Most of us are deeply defined by and identified with the work we do and the titles we hold. We often get confused about how our careers intersect with our faith and our calling. But our careers are just the setting in which we live out our calling to serve as Christ's ambassadors.

The critical thing to keep straight is that our Christian calling to serve God in this life sits above our careers or occupations. Ultimately, we have one job, our holy calling, our new identity, and the single task he has given us to do. God has given us this one job, and it takes precedence over every other priority. In simple terms, that job is to know, love, and serve Christ by joining in his kingdom revolution to transform the world. That starts by surrendering to him.

Surrendered leaders have immense influence because they have nothing left to lose—they've already put everything in God's hands. There's nothing left to fear or protect. A surrendered leader can rise above the daily pressures and stresses of life and work. A surrendered leader is not bound by the same worries, concerns, and priorities that consume others. A surrendered leader is called to a higher purpose: to know God, to love God, and to serve him in this life. A surrendered leader looks and acts differently because it's no longer about them.

Coworkers see a surrendered leader who values the well-being of the people in their care more than the urgent demands of the moment. This kind of leader provokes questions: "Why do you seem different? Why do you care? What makes you tick?" And the answers to those questions are found in the gospel, the good news that God loves them and that they too can embrace something bigger than themselves, something noble and pure and life-giving. This is how we bring Christ to the workplace and how people are drawn into the kingdom of God. This is how institutions and communities are shaped and made more pleasing to Christ. This is how the world changes. This is our one job. Surrendering to his purposes for our lives is not just a one-time event; it's a daily necessity.

REFLECTIONS ON SURRENDER

1. What most resonated with, inspired, or frustrated you in this chapter? Why?

2. Surrender is one of the most difficult acts God calls us to. Most of us don't want to cede control of our lives entirely. What is the most challenging thing for you to surrender? Why?

3. Have you struggled with compartmentalizing your identity as a follower of Jesus Christ and managing other parts, such as your career, apart from God? Why is this such an easy temptation to fall into?

4. God will use any measure to get your attention to surrender. For me, being fired turned out to be the best way, maybe the only way, for God to get my attention. In what ways has God been trying to get your attention to surrender fully to him?

5. Have you ever considered that your real purpose at the place where you work or lead is to serve Jesus Christ by representing his interests there? How would your approach to work differ if you began each day asking how you can better know, love, and serve God in that place today?

6. What changes are you considering in your leadership to surrender more completely to God and his purpose in your life and in his kingdom?

7. How do Jesus' words in Matthew 16:25 change the way you understand the idea of total surrender in your leadership role?

VALUE 2: SACRIFICE

Read chapter four of *Lead Like It Matters to God*.

Key Leadership Principle: We must sacrifice our ambitions for Christ's ambitions for us.

Key Scripture: "As Jesus was walking beside the Sea of Galilee, he saw two brothers, Simon called Peter and his brother Andrew. They were casting a net into the lake, for they were fishermen. 'Come, follow me,' Jesus said, 'and I will send you out to fish for people.' At once they left their nets and followed him." (Matthew 4:18-20)

God wants to repurpose us. When we surrender our lives so he can do that, however, it comes with a cost. At times he will call us to make very real and tangible sacrifices because we are replacing our ambitions with his, our priorities with his, and our dreams with his. This applies to our careers as much as it does to the other dimensions of our lives.

Consider the following two biblical passages when we look at the idea of sacrifice. In Matthew 4, Jesus saw two fishermen, Peter and Andrew, at work and simply invited them: "Come, follow me." Jesus offered them the enigmatic promise that he would repurpose them and make them "fishers of people." But it would cost them their careers.

Their response to his invitation is remarkable: they dropped everything and immediately followed Jesus with no conditions and no questions asked. They understood that following Jesus must take precedence over everything else in their lives. They sacrificed everything to follow Jesus in a higher calling.

But another passage shows us what happened when a man declined Jesus' offer because the sacrifice was too great. In Mark 10, a rich young ruler approached Jesus, wanting to know how to attain eternal life. He was a devout and sincere believer who wanted to do the right thing. Yet when Jesus called on him to make a great sacrifice—to sell everything he had and to give it to the poor—the young man was unwilling and left feeling sad.

Going through the motions of our faith is not the same thing as total commitment. You see, when we seek to follow Jesus, he won't be compartmentalized; he wants everything we have.

"Everything" is a high price to pay, but Jesus doesn't intend to strip us of all we have; he just wants us to acknowledge that everything we have and all we hope for are his to do with as he pleases. We are trusting him with those things by holding them loosely. There's nothing wrong with having career ambitions, wanting a comfortable home, and wanting to enjoy our lives with friends and family. He asks only that we always put him first, above our other priorities, and that we make all we have and all we are available to him.

If you are open to God's will for your life, it may take you somewhere you don't want to go. God will probably never ask you to literally sell everything you have and give it to the poor. But he does wants you to take everything you have and all that you are and lay those things at his feet for him to do with them—and with you—as he chooses, just as the potter shapes the clay into something more useful and pleasing. It requires us to sacrifice our ambitions in exchange for Christ's ambitions for us, trusting him as he shapes and works the clay of our lives toward his purposes.

REFLECTIONS ON SACRIFICE

1. What most resonated with, inspired, or frustrated you in this chapter? Why?

2. Comfort, wealth, and ambitions are easy to cling to. But if God asked you today to sacrifice your career and walk away from everything you have worked for, what would cause you to hesitate?

3. Think about a time God asked you to sacrifice something precious to you. What was it? Did you respond like Peter and Andrew or like the rich young ruler? What was the outcome?

4. Often when we consider sacrifice, we think about what we're giving up rather than what we are gaining. What losses do you anticipate you might face? What might you gain? When I left my corporate job to come to World Vision, I sacrificed money and title but gained a deeper sense of purpose, a global network of Christian colleagues, a deeper sense of closeness to God, and the great satisfaction of doing something that helped the poorest children on the planet. As you think about the idea of sacrifice, how might that play into your role as a leader?

5. Based on the biblical passages we looked at, how would you say that sacrifice might lead to success? In what ways?

VALUE 3: TRUST

Read chapter five of *Lead Like It Matters to God*.

Key Leadership Principle: Only by learning to trust God for their careers can leaders truly rise above the daily stresses and pressures of life and bear fruit for the Lord.

Key Scripture:

"But blessed is the one who trusts in the LORD,
  whose confidence is in him.
They will be like a tree planted by the water
  that sends out its roots by the stream.
It does not fear when heat comes;
  its leaves are always green.
It has no worries in a year of drought
  and never fails to bear fruit." (Jeremiah 17:7-8)

Trusting God completely is one of the most difficult things we are ever asked to do. But only by trusting God can we rise above the daily stresses and pressures of life and work. And it's when we manage to rise above these pressures that our coworkers see a different kind of leader—a leader who isn't rattled by what rattles everyone else.

Perhaps the best example of this mindset is Jesus himself. Jesus was calm, focused, and totally dependent on God his Father. And people followed him. He exuded a kind of peace and confidence that was as attractive as it was unusual. That's the way God wants us to live in relationship with him—as children trusting our Father.

One of the things people notice about a leader who trusts God is that they are able to remain calm in the face of adversity because they have a larger perspective on the daily turbulence of the workplace. Our faith can and should provide us with a healthier perspective on the inevitable workplace crises.

When Christians compartmentalize their faith from their work, they enter the workplace not as a tree with roots by the stream, as we read in Jeremiah's passage, but like a tumbleweed, blown about by every crisis, out of touch with our life-giving God and unable to rise above worry to bear fruit where they are planted.

Trusting God in the good times is a lot easier than trusting him in the hard times. But God will use those hard times to deepen your trust and reliance on him alone.

REFLECTIONS ON TRUST

1. What most resonated with, inspired, or frustrated you in this chapter? Why?

2. In what area(s) of your life are you most resistant to trusting God? Why?

3. Many times in my career I muttered, "This too shall pass. In ten years when we look back, this crisis won't have mattered." In what ways does that mentality help you to trust God more?

4. If you were able to trust God completely for your career and your finances, how would your attitude and behavior change in your workplace?

5. Think about a time God asked you to trust him with something that seemed impossible. What happened?

PUT THESE VALUES INTO PRACTICE

1. A surrendered leader understands that we are to know, love, and serve God in this life—no matter where we are or in what circumstance we find ourselves. As you seek to surrender yourself fully to God and his purpose for you and for those you lead, pray this prayer as I did every morning: "Lord, I am so grateful for this work you have given me to do. Thank you! Today, show me how I can know, love, and serve you here in this place. I am here for one purpose—to know, love, and serve you in the midst of the other people you have placed here with me." Then keep yourself open to the opportunities that arise out of that prayer.

2. Sacrifice is scary. We are stepping obediently into the unknown and trusting God to take care of us. But when we sacrifice in small things and see God's faithfulness, it builds our trust so that when God calls us to sacrifice something big, we can be more willing to take the risk. This week, look closely at those you lead. Ask God to prompt you to sacrifice something small for someone in your group. It may be to keep your opinion to

yourself in a meeting so you can better listen to the insight of others. It may be to avoid taking credit for an idea so that others can be lifted up.

3. As I stated previously, one of the things people notice about a leader who trusts God is that they are able to remain calm in the face of adversity because they have a larger perspective on the daily turbulence of the workplace. This week, when a challenging task arises for your team or when potential conflict shows itself, start by trusting God to handle the situation. Encourage your team—see them first as humans precious to God. Encourage them and help them see past the trauma of the moment.

EXCELLENCE AND LOVE

Read chapter six of *Lead Like It Matters to God.*

Key Leadership Principle: Excellence is not about winning; it's about producing the best result we are capable of achieving.

Key Scripture: "Whatever you do, work at it with all your heart, as working for the Lord, not for human masters, since you know that you will receive an inheritance from the Lord as a reward. It is the Lord Christ you are serving." (Colossians 3:23-24)

Though the values leaders embrace are more important than the success they achieve, *outcomes do matter*. It's important for us to understand, though, that good outcomes do not lead to excellence; excellence leads to good outcomes.

We need to reward excellence. We can't always control the outcomes of our work, but we can control the effort we put forth and celebrate those who work with diligence. A commitment to excellence simply means that we will strive to do our very best and expect the same of others. This leads to a culture that rewards effort above outcome. In Christian terms, excellence means that we always strive to use the gifts and abilities God has given us to the fullest extent possible.

When you think about it, the understanding that "all we can do is the best we can do" is incredibly liberating. If our best efforts fail, then they fail—no regrets. Once we have done our best, we can have a clear conscience and accept the outcome.

When our emphasis is on making our best effort, we can still celebrate the efforts of the individual or the team, even in the midst of a failure. If we praise a person's best efforts, even though the person didn't achieve a successful outcome, they become motivated to continue to offer their best efforts.

A focus solely on outcomes can lead to a *shame culture*, while a focus on best efforts creates a *celebration culture*. In a shame culture, people are blamed for poor outcomes even when they have worked tirelessly and done their best. When leaders create a celebration culture, they are using positive motivation by rewarding the right behaviors.

Creating a culture of excellence is central to our Christian values. If we are Christ's ambassadors in our workplaces and communities, the stakes are high. We are called to do our best because we carry with us the very reputation of Christ. That's why the apostle Paul urged us toward excellence when he wrote Colossians 3:23-24.

Striving for excellence above outcomes will release the pent-up potential in our people by creating a culture that celebrates excellence and embraces accountability to be the very best.

REFLECTIONS ON EXCELLENCE

1. What most resonated with, inspired, or frustrated you in this chapter? Why?

2. What is the difference between rewarding successful outcomes and rewarding excellence? In what ways have you confused them in the past?

3. In the parable of the talents in Matthew 25, the master judges each of the three servants on the basis of both their different levels of ability and their level of effort. If you applied this to the team members you are leading, what would you do differently?

4. Have you ever succumbed to the "perform or perish" leadership approach to delivering bottom-line outcomes? If so, why? How did that affect the group you were leading?

5. How should we define excellence from a biblical perspective? What are our biblical motives for pursuing excellence? How might those affect or change the way we lead?

6. In what ways can creating a celebration culture change the environment of your team or workplace and encourage excellence?

VALUE 5: LOVE

Read chapter seven of *Lead Like It Matters to God.*

Key Leadership Principle: Jesus calls us to love our neighbors as ourselves, and that includes our coworkers. When people see that their leader truly cares about them, it creates a relationship of trust, fosters a positive culture, and amplifies that leader's witness for Christ.

Key Scripture: "Love is patient, love is kind. It does not envy, it does not boast, it is not proud. It does not dishonor others, it is not self-seeking, it is not easily angered, it keeps no record of wrongs. Love does not delight in evil but rejoices with the truth. It always protects, always trusts, always hopes, always perseveres." (1 Corinthians 13:4-7)

Most of us don't think much about love when we think about important leadership qualities. Yet love has everything to do with how effective and strong we will be as leaders. If we want to be effective ambassadors for Christ in our workplaces, we need to see the people we work with from God's perspective—as people he loves, people for whom Jesus literally gave his life. Moreover, when those people look at us, they need to see a person who truly cares about them. Why? Because we can have no more powerful witness to the truth of the gospel than Christ's love shining through us. We are to be the tangible demonstration of the love, character, and truth of Christ as we live out our faith in full view of others.

Our "job" is to love God and other people—always. To be clear, we don't love people with the touchy-feely, soft love that is so popular in our culture. If we want to know what true love looks like in action, we need only look at 1 Corinthians 13, which is a favorite reading for weddings. Perhaps we should read it at board and staff meetings, as it is also a startling description of what love ought to look like in a leader.

As a Christian leader, your coworkers should be among the main objects of your love. You look out for them, you treat them with care, you want the best for them, and you are even willing to put their interests ahead of your own. It's about showing people—even those you would consider unlovable or enemies—that you value and respect them. When you show the people around you that you care, you earn the right to be their leader. People begin to respect and trust you when they see that you care about them, their ideas, their opinions, their aspirations, and their lives inside and outside the workplace.

A loving leader does not place value labels on people. The janitor is as worthy of care and respect as the CEO. And the CEO is just another person who needs God's love as much as anyone else.

Last, one of your key responsibilities as a leader is to help the people under your care realize their God-given potential. Take time to understand their hopes and aspirations. The best leaders help people achieve the things that are important to them through coaching, encouragement, and providing practical direction.

Jesus' command to love our neighbors as ourselves is one of the hardest things to consistently obey—especially where we work. Nevertheless, Jesus commands us to love our coworkers. First John 4:8 reminds us that "God is love." If God is love, we can ask ourselves the more tangible question "What would *love* do?" in every situation. When you are about to give someone a difficult performance review, ask "What would *love* say?" When someone makes a mistake in their work, how would *love* react? When revenues are declining, profits are down, and staff are anxious, how would *love* behave? When one of your employees discovers they have cancer, what would *love* require?

REFLECTIONS ON LOVE

1. What most resonated with, inspired, or frustrated you in this chapter? Why?

2. Have you ever thought about your leadership responsibility including loving the people you lead? Is it an uncomfortable ideal? Why or why not?

3. At World Vision I had to have a paradigm shift about loving the people I was helping. I realized that once you love someone, everything else flows from that. Looking through this lens, list several things you might start doing and stop doing in your approach to leadership.

4. Think about the most unlovable people you work with. Jesus says that love even extends to them. In what tangible ways can you reach out to love them this week? How often do you pray for the unlovable people you work with? What might those prayers include?

5. When you look at someone, do you have a "glass half empty" or a "glass half full" attitude toward them? Do you tend to see a person's flaws and shortcomings first, or their better attributes? What can you do to change that attitude to be more loving so they feel valued and respected?

6. How much time do you put into getting to know the people on your team? Do you know the names of their kids? Do you know what's going on in their lives outside work, or what their passions are? What would it take for you to spend time seeing them more than just as one-dimensional workers?

PUT THESE VALUES INTO PRACTICE

1. This week, think of ways that you can encourage a celebration culture to move people to strive toward doing their best. This may be such a different approach that it will take people some time to adjust. But as you lead by example, take note of how your people begin to change their work ethic and mentality.

2. Before you show up at work tomorrow and every morning, recite these words: "As a leader I am patient, I am kind. I do not envy, I do not boast, I am not proud. I do not dishonor others, I am not self-seeking, I am not easily angered, I keep no record of wrongs. I do not delight in evil but rejoice with the truth. I always protect, always trust, always hope, always persevere." Then work to live up to those words, which have the power to positively impact every encounter you have for the rest of the day.

3. In Luke 6, Jesus talked about loving our enemies, that we must do good and bless those who mistreat or hate us. Think of that person in your office who fits the description of an "enemy." Instead of paying back insult for insult and offense with offense, try interacting with them in a positive and caring way—the same way you might treat someone who is kind and affirming toward you. Pray for them and, as much as it depends on you, treat them with a kind spirit.

3

HUMILITY AND INTEGRITY

VALUE 6: HUMILITY

Read chapter eight of *Lead Like It Matters to God*.

Key Leadership Principle: A leader with humility understands that it isn't about them. The humble leader listens to the input of others, encourages competing points of view, values all members of their team, and seeks the welfare of others over self.

Key Scripture: "Do nothing out of selfish ambition or vain conceit. Rather, in humility value others above yourselves, not looking to your own interests but each of you to the interests of the others." (Philippians 2:3-4)

For leaders, the sin of pride can too often easily rear its ugly head as they experience success. This is why humility in a leader is an all-too-rare quality. In *The Purpose Driven Life*, Rick Warren wrote, "True humility is not thinking less of yourself; it is thinking of yourself less." This suggests that humility does not require us to deny the positive gifts and talents we possess, but rather that we need to recognize that God gave us those gifts and talents for a purpose.

As Christian leaders, our first responsibility is not to be a superstar; it is to seek the well-being of the people we are entrusted to lead and to bring out the best in them. That is impossible to accomplish if we are at war within ourselves for our own success and prosperity. Leadership always comes with power, and power has a way of going to our heads. Pride can easily take root in the soil of leadership. And pride disconnects us from God.

Humble leaders seek their team's success. Prideful leaders listen only to their own counsel, while humble leaders listen to the counsel of many. Prideful leaders see other people as a means to their desired ends, but humble leaders see the welfare of their people as an end in itself.

How do we embrace humility? It begins by saying, "Not my will, Lord, but your will. How can I better know, love, and serve you in the place you have put me?"

God isn't impressed with our strength. He wants us humbled and totally dependent on him in our weakness. As Paul wrote in 1 Corinthians 12:9, "'My grace is sufficient for you, for my power is made perfect in weakness.' Therefore, I will boast all the more gladly about my weaknesses, so that Christ's power may rest on me." Only then do we have full access to God's power working through us.

REFLECTIONS ON HUMILITY

1. What most resonated with, inspired, or frustrated you in this chapter? Why?

2. What does it mean to put the interests of others ahead of our own? What are some obstacles to this?

3. Think about a time or circumstance you sought the attention and acceptance of others. Why did you desire that praise from them?

4. A humble leader recognizes that they do not possess all the gifts and abilities needed for their team to be successful. Think of one or two people on your team at work and list the specific talents and abilities they have that you might be lacking.

5. What safeguards have you placed around yourself, or plan to place around yourself, to ensure that you can avoid the temptations of power, success, and self-importance?

VALUE 7: INTEGRITY

Read chapter nine of *Lead Like It Matters to God*.

Key Leadership Principle: Integrity is one of the most powerful values a leader can possess and the bedrock of a leader's credibility. It creates a cascade of positive outcomes for a team or an organization, including trust, unity, motivation, and improved morale and productivity.

Key Scripture:

"Who may worship in your sanctuary, LORD?
    Who may enter your presence on your holy hill?
Those who lead blameless lives and do what is right,
    speaking the truth from sincere hearts.
Those who refuse to gossip
    or harm their neighbors
    or speak evil of their friends.

Those who despise flagrant sinners,
>   and honor the faithful followers of the LORD,
>   and keep their promises even when it hurts.
> Those who lend money without charging interest,
>   and who cannot be bribed to lie about the innocent.
> Such people will stand firm forever." (Psalm 15:1-5 NLT)

It has been said that "integrity is doing the right thing, even when no one is watching." In other words, a leader's private behavior is a good predictor of their true nature. If their private behavior is honest and ethical, it is likely that their public behavior can be trusted as well. This has always been one of the litmus tests for integrity because it speaks to the consistency of one's character. And here is a universal truth: everyone appreciates and values coworkers and bosses who demonstrate integrity.

We can break down integrity into three categories: personal, relational, and corporate integrity.

Integrity is the moral and ethical compass, the North Star that allows a leader to navigate any and every situation with the confidence that they are traveling in the right direction. A leader with integrity provides her staff with the confidence that she will always strive to do the right thing, the fair thing, even if it's costly or difficult. She keeps her word and treats people with respect. Integrity is a kind of super-quality because when a leader consistently demonstrates integrity, it results in a cascade of positive outcomes: it builds trust, diminishes fear and anxiety, improves employee morale and customer satisfaction, and increases productivity.

When we think of a lack of integrity, we tend to think first about things like lying, stealing, or cheating. But integrity is a much broader concept. The whole area of relational integrity influences all our interactions with others. Integrity in our relationships requires that we deal with others honestly, sincerely, transparently, considerately, and fairly.

People should feel safe with us, knowing that we will never try to use them to our advantage. They should feel that they can trust us, count on us, and confide in us.

For a Christian, integrity is foundational to our faith and a requirement of our commitment to God that we will live according to his teachings. If we are to be effective ambassadors for Christ in our workplaces—our "one job"—we must be people of integrity. In 2 Corinthians 8:21, Paul speaks of the importance of doing the right thing, not just because God is pleased, but because other people are watching us: "We are taking pains to do what is right, not only in the eyes of the Lord but also in the eyes of man."

Jesus told us in Matthew 5:16, "Make your light shine, so that others will see the good that you do and will praise your Father in heaven" (CEV). We have the privilege of reflecting the light of Christ in our workplaces and communities. We have the opportunity to shine our lights in places that are sometimes dark, to be a presence of calm in the midst of storms, and to be a voice of reason in stressful situations. That is the power of integrity.

REFLECTIONS ON INTEGRITY

1. What most resonated with, inspired, or frustrated you in this chapter? Why?

2. In what ways does relational integrity and lack of relational integrity affect your workplace?

3. Think about a leader who has impressed you with their personal integrity. What specifically about that person displayed that character trait?

4. Broken relationships and grudges can cripple a workplace. Are there people in your workplace that you dislike, avoid, or disparage to others? How could you restore a healthier working relationship with them?

5. Corporate integrity speaks to the culture of an organization. In thinking about your place of work, how would you rate its corporate integrity? What are the factors that make that culture either positive or negative in this dimension? What could you do to positively influence that culture?

6. Think about a time or situation in which you could have compromised your integrity. What was it and what did you do?

PUT THESE VALUES INTO PRACTICE

1. Make a plan this week to seek accountability. Ask two people you trust to reveal specific areas in your leadership in which they see you displaying pride. Listen with an open mind and then strategize ways you can rid yourself of pride and lift others up.

2. As you lead others, give them permission to challenge your thinking and disagree with you when they believe they have a better idea. It has been my experience that people are always intimidated by the boss. They are not likely to take the risk of disagreeing with you unless they feel completely safe doing so. Start your next meeting by announcing that you want to hear everyone's opinions and that you hope the group can have an open debate about the issues you're going to discuss. Surround yourself with smart people, give them permission to challenge you, and show them that you value what they have to say. Be sure to give them credit when their contributions make a difference.

3. Make a list of people in your workplace you have trouble with—people you may dislike or with whom you may have a grudge. Determine at least one positive step or action you can take in those relationships to improve them and then take that step. It could be as simple as paying them a compliment or as serious as apologizing for something you did. Reflect on how they respond.

VISION AND COURAGE

VALUE 8: VISION

Read chapter ten of *Lead Like It Matters to God*.

Key Leadership Principle: One of the chief tasks of a leader is to create a vision for a different and better future and a belief that it can be achieved.

Key Scripture: "Now when Jesus saw the crowds, he went up on a mountainside and sat down. His disciples came to him, and he began to teach them. He said:

'Blessed are the poor in spirit,
   for theirs is the kingdom of heaven.
Blessed are those who mourn,
   for they will be comforted.
Blessed are the meek,
   for they will inherit the earth.
Blessed are those who hunger and thirst for righteousness,
   for they will be filled.
Blessed are the merciful,
   for they will be shown mercy.
Blessed are the pure in heart,
   for they will see God.
Blessed are the peacemakers,
   for they will be called children of God.
Blessed are those who are persecuted because of righteousness,
   for theirs is the kingdom of heaven.'" (Matthew 5:1-10)

Vision, or vision casting, may be one of the most difficult leadership qualities to embody because it calls on a leader to envision the future. A leader has the responsibility to chart the course, provide direction, and set priorities for the group they are leading in order to arrive at some desired future state. But "seeing the future" is like driving a bus at night on a winding road in a snowstorm at seventy miles an hour with no headlights or windshield wipers, while all of the passengers are complaining about your driving skills.

Nevertheless, providing a compelling vision for any organization or endeavor is a crucial element for creating clarity, unity, and motivation. When a team has a clear understanding of where they are now, where they need to go, and what it will take to get there, it provides the clarity they need to pull together to achieve the task.

Since vision casting can seem like some mysterious kind of divination, let's break the visioning process into four parts. A leader must define the current reality, articulate a desired future, identify a way forward, and personally "own" the vision. Defining reality calls for a leader to first have a thorough understanding of the present. A distorted view of reality can have disastrous results, so a vision for a better future begins with a sober assessment of the current reality. Having gained an understanding of that reality, leaders can then more easily articulate the desired future they are aiming for. Once they articulate that vision to their team, they need to strategize a plan, or identify the way forward, and set a course to achieve it. Finally, in order to make that vision the new reality, leaders must "own" it, passionately investing time and energy in it, since the best leaders lead by example.

REFLECTIONS ON VISION

1. What most resonated with, inspired, or frustrated you in this chapter? Why?

2. A vision for a better future begins with a sober assessment of the current reality. Looking at your own organization and your leadership, how would you articulate its current reality in four or five bullet points? How does that help as you cast a vision for those you lead?

3. You can use this four-step visioning process to clarify your own personal walk with the Lord. Go through these four steps to articulate and realize a "desired future" for living out your faith at work.

4. Describe a time you worked to cast a fresh vision with your team. What were some of your struggles in getting everyone on board? Looking at the four part of a vision-casting process, which did you neglect to spend enough time in? Do you think that made a difference?

5. For "extra credit" read through the Sermon on the Mount (Matthew 5–7) and note some of the ways Jesus challenged and redefined the status quo. What are one or two things he did or said during his ministry that demonstrate how he personally "owned" that new vision?

VALUE 9: COURAGE

Read chapter eleven of *Lead Like It Matters to God*.

Key Leadership Principle: Leaders who demonstrate courage when facing tough challenges and decisions will inspire their teams to overcome their own fears, enabling better performance and greater focus on desired outcomes.

Key Scripture: "Be strong and courageous. Do not be afraid; do not be discouraged, for the LORD your God will be with you wherever you go." (Joshua 1:9)

Leading into the future, even when everyone is on board with the vision you've cast, can create fear—fear of change, fear of taking the wrong course, fear of what might happen. And overcoming those fears requires a leader's courage, as the team will look to you to instill calm and confidence in them.

For the Christian the opposite of fear is not courage but faith. If we believe we are doing the right thing, if we believe we are doing something close to the heart of God, then we can count on God's support. We can trust God for the outcome. Our faith leads to trust, and trust enables courage. Consider Moses, a great example of both fear and courage, who had to approach the most powerful man in the world, Pharaoh, and demand that he release all his Israelite slaves. To Moses it sounded like a suicide mission. Yet God essentially told Moses that he needed faith not courage—faith that God would go with him, protect him, and deliver the outcome. He was simply asking Moses to trust him. And of course, we know that Moses finally, if reluctantly, overcame his fear, obeyed God, and became one of the greatest heroes of the Old Testament. Ultimately, it was his faith that overcame his fear and produced the courage he needed. God could be trusted.

Forty years later, as the Israelites moved into the Promised Land, it was Joshua who needed courage. So God encouraged him, "Be strong and courageous. Do not be afraid; do not be discouraged, for the LORD your God will be with you wherever you go."

It is our faith that enables us to put our fear in perspective. Courage calls us to keep doing the right thing, no matter the consequences, and then to trust God for the outcome. Faith produces trust, and trust enables courage. God's got our back.

REFLECTIONS ON COURAGE

1. What most resonated with, inspired, or frustrated you in this chapter? Why?

2. Make a list of the things at work or in your home life that create the most fear, anxiety, or apprehension in you. Why do you think it is so hard to trust God for those things? What steps could you take to turn them over to him? (Read Philippians 4:6-7; Matthew 6:25-34; 11:28-30.)

3. What are some ways that you have calmed your team's fears and instilled within them a sense of confidence? How did that help to build their trust in you?

4. Describe a time when fear kept you from leading the way you needed to. What happened?

5. How can "owning a vision" that you've cast actually help give more courage to your team? Why do you think that is?

6. Jesus told his followers, including us: "Peace I leave with you; my peace I give you. I do not give to you as the world gives. Do not let your hearts be troubled and do not be afraid" (John 14:27). Does the promise of peace make it easier for you to trust and have courage, particularly in the way you lead? Why or why not?

PUT THESE VALUES INTO PRACTICE

1. If your organization or team already has a vision statement, evaluate it by assessing how well you and your organization stack up on each of the four steps. If your organization or team has no such articulated vision, why not lead your team to develop one?

2. In your workplace, identify the three or four threats, decisions, situations, or individuals that cause you to feel fearful. These fears might be caused by economic, marketplace, interpersonal, situational, cultural, or job-security factors. Use this as a list that you pray through regularly. Ask God to replace your fears with courage, trust, and peace.

5

GENEROSITY AND FORGIVENESS

VALUE 10: GENEROSITY

Read chapter twelve of *Lead Like It Matters to God*.

Key Leadership Principle: Money and the pursuit of money can be corrosive. Leaders who treat money as a means to an end rather than an end in itself can lift the eyes of their team to the higher purpose of their work.

Key Scripture: "Those who want to get rich fall into temptation and a trap and into many foolish and harmful desires that plunge people into ruin and destruction. For the love of money is a root of all kinds of evil. Some people, eager for money, have wandered from the faith and pierced themselves with many griefs. But you, man of God, flee from all this, and pursue righteousness, godliness, faith, love, endurance and gentleness." (1 Timothy 6:9-11)

It is impossible to talk about leadership without discussing the profound influence of money on leaders, the people they manage, and the institutions they lead. The love of money, or greed, can be a cancer in our lives and in the places we work. Yet generosity is the leadership virtue that stands in opposition to greed because a leader characterized by generosity is a person who sees money as a tool, not as an idol.

Scripture is correct in stating that money itself is not the problem but rather the love of money. It is our relationship to money that has the potential to be damaging to our lives and the lives of those around us if we are not careful. The pursuit of money can have all kinds of unintended consequences where we work.

Perhaps most damaging is that *money sometimes replaces purpose* in an organization. Money can become a counterfeit purpose that infiltrates an organization and over time replaces its higher purpose. At first it may be unnoticeable, and the company can continue to perform well. But over time, if a higher purpose isn't lifted up by its leaders, the company becomes a host organism for people who want to extract money from it. And the people who work there become pawns, the means to the end of bigger salaries and bonuses for the executives and shareholders.

The place you work is your place of Christian ministry, and you have been placed there to serve God. So money is not your main purpose for being there; ministry is. Your "one job" is to be an ambassador for Christ in the place you live and work, and you need to be careful not to allow your personal pursuit of money to replace that God-given purpose.

For the Christian leader, having the right perspective on money is critical. We cannot serve both masters, as Jesus tells us in Matthew 6:24. In 1 Timothy 6, Paul explains the danger of money. What does he suggest Timothy do to avoid falling into its trap? "Flee from all this, and pursue righteousness, godliness, faith, love, endurance and gentleness." Paul warns Timothy to run from this love of money and instead pursue Christlike values—in other words, a godly character.

As a leader in your workplace you have an opportunity to be a person who is not "owned" by money. You can put the well-being of people ahead of money. You can focus your efforts and those of your team on higher values like excellence, integrity, perseverance, and diligence, and create a workplace that allows people to flourish. Focus them on the mission of the organization, not just their compensation. Show them that money is your servant, not your master.

REFLECTIONS ON GENEROSITY

1. What most resonated with, inspired, or frustrated you in this chapter? Why?

2. Consider the pervasive influence of money (compensation, financial targets, budgets, expenses, etc.) in your place of work. Share some ways that money creates dysfunction and leads to negative consequences for the organization and the people who work there.

3. What are some ways money might replace purpose in your organization? How does money affect your ability to lead well?

4. When I was struggling over a higher-paying job opportunity, my wife, Reneé, said, "Money is a lousy reason for doing anything. We need to be where God wants us to be and trust him to take care of us." Do you agree? Why or why not?

5. The way we handle our personal finances can affect the way we approach money at work. What role does tithing and giving to the Lord's work play in your family? How does giving money

away create a healthier relationship between you and money? The traditional tithe is 10 percent of your income. If you are giving less than that, what steps might you take to get there?

VALUE 11: FORGIVENESS

Read chapter thirteen of *Lead Like It Matters to God.*

Key Leadership Principle: Apology and forgiveness heal broken relationships and promote organizational health. Leaders need to model forgiveness in the workplace both by offering it and asking for it.

Key Scriptures: "Be kind and compassionate to one another, forgiving each other, just as in Christ God forgave you." (Ephesians 4:32)

"If we claim to be without sin, we deceive ourselves and the truth is not in us." (1 John:1:8)

Forgiveness is central to the Christian story. At the core of our faith is the knowledge that we are broken people, incapable of restoring our relationship with God, or with each other, through our own efforts. And that admission is foundational to understanding and navigating our relationship with God and with those around us—including those in our workplaces.

Our vertical relationship with God can be restored only when we repent of our sins and accept God's forgiveness, made possible through Christ's atoning death. The process goes like this: *sin* → *repentance* → *forgiveness* → *restoration*. Through forgiveness that which was broken becomes whole again. It is restored. And this is also true of our relationships with other people. God's model of forgiveness and restoration can transform the horizontal relationships we have with others—family, friends, spouses, coworkers, and even our enemies.

Christian leaders must conduct themselves with the knowledge that they too are broken and flawed people, both needing forgiveness and willing to forgive others. During the normal course of human interaction in a workplace, people say and do hurtful things, and they make mistakes that affect those around them. Unfortunately, the simple and powerful words, "I'm sorry," are rarely uttered. And they are uttered even more rarely by leaders, perhaps because apology and forgiveness require leaders to be vulnerable—something many are uncomfortable doing.

We cannot control the ways others conduct themselves in our workplaces, but we can control our response to their actions. And that means forgiving people whether they apologize for their words or their behavior or not. By intentionally choosing not to hold grudges, we help reduce bad "cholesterol" that can so easily clog our work relationships. And by doing this we prevent small grudges from escalating into major conflicts.

God calls us to set a high standard for the way we are to respond to those who provoke us and to set the example of repentance and forgiveness for others to model. Apologizing can be healing and restorative. It also makes us less likely to do the same thing again.

Even more powerful is when a leader apologizes for a mistake or a harsh word in a more public setting. People deeply appreciate a vulnerable leader who is willing to admit their mistakes and own them with integrity. And it helps create a culture where everyone becomes accountable for their occasional mistakes or bad behavior.

Apology does not come easily to most of us because it necessitates that we admit we have done something wrong. It requires raw vulnerability to humble ourselves before the person or persons to whom we are apologizing. And it is especially hard for a leader to apologize because it involves submission and admitting weakness. But it is the only thing that has the power to restore a broken trust or relationship. A leader who understands the need for forgiveness and the power of apology is a leader whom others will seek to follow.

REFLECTIONS ON FORGIVENESS

1. What most resonated with, inspired, or frustrated you in this chapter? Why?

2. Why do you think it is so difficult for people to ask for forgiveness when they have done something wrong? Do you struggle with offering apologies and forgiveness? Why or why not?

3. Are apologies and forgiveness common or rare at your workplace? Why do you think that is?

4. Think about the worst leadership mistake or decision you made. What was it? How did you come clean and apologize for it? If you didn't apologize, what kept you from that? Looking back on it now, what would you have done differently in terms of seeking forgiveness?

5. Describe a time (at work or in a personal relationship) when you offered or received an apology. In what ways did it bring restoration?

6. Why is it important to forgive coworkers even if they don't ask you for it?

7. In what ways does remembering how God forgives us help us to forgive others and to seek forgiveness more intentionally? (Read Matthew 18:21-35.)

PUT THESE VALUES INTO PRACTICE

1. If your organization or team struggles with replacing purpose for money, then create a plan to help refocus the organization on its core values and higher purpose. Work on creating a mission statement to give your team a greater sense of pride in what they do. Lifting employees' sights to this higher purpose can give them a renewed sense of pride in the company. Though making money is essential to any company, it doesn't have to be the main purpose.

2. Become more intentional about forgiveness this week. If you've lost your temper with someone or made a mistake, pull that person aside later and apologize. Make forgiveness—both requesting it and offering it—an established part of your leadership and work culture. Be quick to seek forgiveness by just saying something as simple as "I'm sorry for _____."

SELF-AWARENESS AND BALANCE

Read chapter fourteen of *Lead Like It Matters to God*.

Key Leadership Principle: The best leaders make efforts to become aware of their own weaknesses and shortcomings and learn to understand the magnified impact their words and actions can have on others.

Key Scripture: "Why do you look at the speck of sawdust in your brother's eye and pay no attention to the plank in your own eye?" (Matthew 7:3)

The best leaders make efforts to become aware of their own weaknesses and shortcomings and to learn to understand the magnified impact their words and actions can have on others. That's because the best leaders take the thoughts and feelings of other people into account. Self-awareness is complex and has three different dimensions: *Role awareness* is about understanding your unique role as a leader. *Personal awareness* is a knowledge of one's own strengths and weaknesses, talents, and deficiencies. *Relational awareness* is about understanding how others see us.

Perception versus reality is a tricky concept. We often say and do things with one intent, but others perceive them differently from how we intend. In a workplace, the perception-versus-reality problem can become magnified by power, position, and money. The people under a leader's authority are keenly aware that their leader has power and authority. This power imbalance has a way of distorting and magnifying the words that come from a leader's mouth, often with unintended consequences. Self-aware leaders learn to understand the magnified impact of their actions and words.

A crucial component of a leader's self-awareness is to recognize that stereotypes can profoundly and detrimentally distort workplace dynamics. All of us see the world through our unique lens, influenced by our age, race, gender, cultural, spiritual and economic background, and upbringing. We may be unaware of our biases, which is how they can distort and hobble our leadership in unhealthy ways. When we prejudge people based on things like gender, race, nationality—even height, weight, or appearance—we fail to leverage the wonderful diversity of gifts and talents God has placed around us.

As Jesus told us, we must remove the plank in our eye (that is, become more self-aware) before we turn to address a speck in someone else's. If we want to "see clearly," we must start with self-awareness; we first must acknowledge and remove the "plank" from our own eye. In other words, before we judge others—or lead them—we need to take a long, hard look at our own shortcomings and motives. Only when we have done a fair assessment of our own deficiencies are we in the proper state of mind to "see clearly" those of our coworkers.

REFLECTIONS ON SELF-AWARENESS

1. What most resonated with, inspired, or frustrated you in this chapter? Why?

2. How might your words and actions as a leader impact others in negative ways?

3. Think about the three dimensions of self-awareness. Describe a person you have worked with who lacked self-awareness in each of those dimensions. How did that person act? How did this make you and others feel?

4. Now think about your own self-awareness. In which of those three dimensions do you struggle the most? Why? What would help you become more self-aware in that area?

5. All of us have strengths and weaknesses. Do you have an accurate sense of your own abilities and weaknesses? Make a list of both your strongest and weakest "suits" in your workplace role. How might you compensate for those weaker suits?

6. Think of a time when your words or actions might have impacted someone negatively in your workplace. What specifically

made you realize it? Did you do anything to make it right? If not, what could you have done?

VALUE 13: BALANCE

Read chapter fifteen of *Lead Like It Matters to God*.

Key Leadership Principle: A leader who achieves a healthy balance in life between work, family, faith, and rest will broaden their perspective, make better decisions, and set a positive example for their teams.

Key Scriptures: "Very early in the morning, while it was still dark, Jesus got up, left the house and went off to a solitary place, where he prayed. Simon and his companions went to look for him, and when they found him, they exclaimed: 'Everyone is looking for you!'" (Mark 1:35-37)

"Jesus often withdrew to lonely places and prayed." (Luke 5:15-16)

In today's work environment, where connectivity is 24-7, establishing boundaries between work and life is exceedingly difficult. Work follows you home every day, stays with you on the weekends, and even goes on vacation with you. You're often expected to be available at all hours to answer emails, texts, and phone calls. The result can be a blurring of life and work, which can be both stressful and harmful in the long run. It calls for establishing healthy boundaries.

Sometimes that just involves you making healthier choices, but if the demands are out of your control, it requires you to have a difficult conversation with your boss about your workload and his or her expectations of you. You also have a responsibility to help those under your supervision achieve an acceptable work-life balance in their lives by agreeing on reasonable boundaries.

There is another cause of poor work-life balance that is not externally imposed but self-imposed: workaholism. In the high-pressure culture found in many work environments, the workaholic becomes a kind of tragic hero. He or she is the person who sacrifices anything for the cause. Essentially, a workaholic exchanges short-term gains in their work for long-term tragedies in their lives as they become consumed by the "tyranny of the urgent." At its core, workaholism is a form of self-importance that believes that "nobody else can do it if I'm not involved." That attitude sends a terrible message to the team you are leading—that they just aren't good enough to do it without you. And your poor example will put pressure on them to adopt your damaging work habits. The best leaders leverage the gifts and abilities of the entire team so that no single individual has to carry an inordinate share of the work.

The opposite of the workaholic is the balanced leader. Balance means a lot more than just spending time with your family, though that is critically important. A balanced life is a well-rounded life in multiple dimensions. For leaders to be at their best, they need to have clear minds, stability outside the workplace, positive relationships with both family and friends, and a sense of meaning and purpose not solely derived from work.

For the Christian leader, purpose and identity are found first in our relationship with God and our "one job" to know, love, and serve him in this life. As Christ's ambassadors, we are "on mission" in our workplaces. That means we need to make adequate time for worship, prayer, Scripture, devotions, and service. These things remind us of who we belong to and connect us to the deeper purpose and meaning of our work.

In Mark 1 we see one of the many times Jesus withdrew from his "work" to spend time in prayer, reconnecting with his Father in heaven. Jesus understood that his mission was so critical that he had to make time to get away from the demands placed on him so he could align himself with the Father's purposes. Jesus was seeking balance in his life. In the same way we, as Christ's ambassadors, must also withdraw from the many stresses to align with the Father's purposes. If we are spiritually out of balance, everything else in our lives will be negatively affected.

But achieving balance in our lives only starts with our "God time." It also requires that we make time for family, friendships, service, reading, rest, and recreation. And this kind of diversification has another important benefit for leaders: it gives us a broader perspective on the bigger picture and our higher purpose.

REFLECTIONS ON BALANCE

1. What most resonated with, inspired, or frustrated you in this chapter? Why?

2. There was an illustration in this chapter about filling a jar with walnuts and rice—the walnuts representing life's highest priorities and the rice representing all the other demands on your life (see "What Are Your Walnuts?" in chapter fifteen in *Lead Like It Matters to God*). When the rice was put in first, there wasn't enough room for the walnuts, but when the walnuts went in first, the rice seemed to fit in as well, filling the spaces between the walnuts. Make a list, in order of priority, of the "walnuts" in your life. Then make a list of the things that represent the "rice." Are there things in your life that you need to move from one category to the other?

3. Achieving work-life balance inevitably requires you to resolve competing and conflicting priorities. In your life, what conflicts are causing the most tension? Can you articulate some strategies and boundaries that would help ease those tensions and create more harmony? What might be the consequences of doing this—or not doing it?

4. As a leader, you have both the opportunity and the responsibility to help your team manage their work-life tensions satisfactorily. How involved are you with staff as they try to navigate those tensions? What tangible steps could you take as a leader to help your team members achieve a healthier balance? (These might differ by team member.)

5. Achieving balance in our lives starts with our "God time." It also requires that we make time for family, friendships, service, reading, rest, and recreation. Rate on a scale of one to five, with one being the least, how you are doing with each of these categories. Which is the easiest for you? Which is the most difficult? Why?

PUT THESE VALUES INTO PRACTICE

1. If you've never subjected yourself to a 360-degree review, in which you are confidentially evaluated by a group of your co-workers, initiate one. It will give you a candid glimpse into exactly how others perceive you. Though it will feel uncomfortable, since most likely you will hear some criticism, it will give you a good indication of how self-aware you are and what steps you need to take to make positive strides forward. You might even include your family! Allow them to freely share how your work is affecting your home life.

2. If you are leading a team, schedule a private meeting with each member to specifically ask how they are managing the work-life balance. Ask them what aspects of the job put the greatest stress on their lives outside work. Then ask them what changes you could make to help. You may be surprised that just a few compromises might dramatically help them—and result in happier, healthier, and more motivated team members.

3. Look over your schedule for this week and next. Apart from any urgent matters, where can you incorporate balance? Create an "ideal" schedule, blocking out times that will allow you to give adequate time for the essentials: God, family, friends, rest, work, and so on. For the next week or so, stick to that ideal schedule. Evaluate how you feel at the end of that time. Tweak as needed to incorporate more balance, and then—with no apologies—stick with it.

7

HUMOR AND ENCOURAGEMENT

Read chapter sixteen of *Lead Like It Matters to God*.

Key Leadership Principle: A leader who uses humor well has a powerful culture-shaping tool that can ease tension, relieve stress, and bring a healthy perspective to workplace challenges. Humor is a gift you can give to those you lead.

Key Scripture:

"There is a time for everything,
> and a season for every activity under the heavens . . .
> a time to weep and a time to laugh,
> a time to mourn and a time to dance." (Ecclesiastes 3:1, 4)

Humor is a powerful tool in a leader's tool kit. It builds camaraderie and team spirit. In the midst of difficulty, it can bring relief and a healthier outlook. It helps us face our most difficult challenges without despairing. Humor helps us put problems and situations in perspective. It provides us a coping mechanism when we are overwhelmed. And as a leader, humor is a gift you can give to those you lead.

A leader who uses humor puts people at ease. Humor can break the ice in a meeting where people are not well acquainted because it taps into our universal human experience. A team who can laugh together is in a better frame of mind to work together with trust and shared purpose.

Though humor is important, we have to be careful with it. Humor in the workplace has to be gentle and not biting. And, as Christians, we must resist the temptation to fall into the vulgar humor and language that characterize many secular work environments. Indulging in that kind of coarseness will undermine our efforts to demonstrate the character of Christ to our coworkers.

Humor can be uplifting, but it can also be weaponized to hurt people. If you use humor to embarrass or humiliate a coworker, it can be devastating, especially if you are the boss. Make the humor about the situation or circumstances your team finds themselves in. Your humor should be good-hearted. Even better if you can poke fun at yourself and show that you don't take yourself too seriously. Self-deprecating humor makes a leader more human, more approachable, and more relatable to the people on their team.

Laughter is desperately needed. It is therapy, restorative. People are hungry for an occasional laugh that can bring them needed relief in the everyday stresses of the work environment.

REFLECTIONS ON HUMOR

1. What most resonated with, inspired, or frustrated you in this chapter? Why?

2. Why do you think humor is an important trait for a leader to have and use wisely?

3. Some of the best humor is self-deprecating, when leaders poke fun at themselves and show that they don't take themselves too seriously. Describe a time when you or another leader offered that kind of humor. How did the coworkers respond? Did it lighten the morale of the group?

4. Humor needs to be gentle, especially in a work atmosphere. Describe a time when a leader or coworker used humor in a coarse or derogatory way. What lesson can you learn from that experience?

5. Not everyone is a natural at humor, but everyone can use humor in ways that fit their personality. You might be that person who has an easy and natural running monologue, or maybe you're someone with a much drier and more restrained sense of humor. Both can work. Ask yourself how you might specifically use humor in your work environment to relieve stress and build camaraderie.

VALUE 15: ENCOURAGEMENT

Read chapter seventeen of *Lead Like It Matters to God*.

Key Leadership Principle: A leader who understands the power of encouragement and affirmation will see a huge return on investment, paid back in improved performance, motivation, and loyalty.

Key Scripture: "Encourage one another and build each other up, just as in fact you are doing. Now we ask you, brothers and sisters, to acknowledge those who work hard among you, who care for you in the Lord and who admonish you. Hold them in the highest regard in love because of their work." (1 Thessalonians 5:11-13)

The best leaders know that regular affirmation and encouragement, not criticism, is what helps the people on their team develop confidence, improve their performance, and lean into their gifts and abilities. Encouragement energizes people, while criticism often demoralizes. Good leaders understand the power of encouragement to motivate others, lift performance, and help the people around them realize their full, God-given potential.

The starting point for understanding the power of encouragement in our workplaces is how we view the people with whom we work. If we see them as uniquely and wonderfully made, with attributes and qualities given to them by their Creator, we can begin to unleash the remarkable abilities God has vested in them. When we embrace this view of our coworkers, encouragement flows more naturally from our lips.

When you as the leader emphasize and praise positive attributes and behaviors, your coworker walks away energized and encouraged, with greater confidence in their ability to contribute to the team. Encouragement is free, it costs you nothing, but it will deliver a huge return on investment. And it works at all levels. You can encourage people below you, above you, and across from you in the organization. People like that give you energy and confidence. Be one of them and surround yourself with people who are encouragers.

REFLECTIONS ON ENCOURAGEMENT

1. What most resonated with, inspired, or frustrated you in this chapter? Why?

2. What does it mean that encouragement is all about using the carrot more often than the stick? How have you seen the truth of this?

3. Think back on your life and how it turned out the way it did. Are there moments that stand out when positive encouragement made a huge difference in your self-confidence?

4. Stephen Covey once said, "Treat a man as he is and he will remain as he is. Treat a man as he can and should be and he will become as he can and should be." When have you found that to be true in your workplace or perhaps in your own life? Explain.

5. In my various leadership roles over the years, I too often fell into the mindset of criticism when managing my people. What has been your default response in leadership? Do you err on the side of criticism or encouragement? Why?

6. When someone on your team consistently fails to carry out their responsibilities despite your affirmation and encouragement, you may have to make the tough decision to remove them from their job. How might you do that while still helping them maintain their dignity and self-worth?

PUT THESE VALUES INTO PRACTICE

1. Practice some self-deprecating humor this week—it takes some good-natured humility! When you stumble, make light of it. If you aren't a humorous person by nature, find jokes or funny stories off the internet and share them (making sure they're clean and kind, using unoffensive humor). Practice self-awareness when offering humor so that you aren't unintentionally making someone the butt of a joke and hurting them.

2. While criticism has its place, it is better received when cloaked in praise. For the next month, make a concerted effort to look for opportunities to affirm and encourage your team members both publicly and privately. And when you need to offer a critical word, frame it within the context of your coworker's positive qualities. Also, send a few brief "just because" notes of encouragement. When your coworker in another department does something well, tell them how much you appreciate them. When your boss does something great, affirm them. When the month is over, see if you notice a difference in these relationships.

PERSEVERANCE AND LISTENING

VALUE 16: PERSEVERANCE

Read chapter eighteen of *Lead Like It Matters to God.*

Key Leadership Principle: When a leader exhibits perseverance and grit in the face of difficult challenges, it sustains hope and lifts the confidence of their entire team.

Key Scripture: "Consider it pure joy, my brothers and sisters, whenever you face trials of many kinds, because you know that the testing of your faith produces perseverance. Let perseverance finish its work so that you may be mature and complete, not lacking anything." (James 1:2-4)

In *Good to Great*, Jim Collins states that the best leaders of the most successful companies in America are individuals who are characterized by a deep sense of personal humility and who exhibit a dogged commitment to persevere in the face of challenges and adversity. Collins calls them Level 5 leaders. Perseverance requires a refusal to give up, no matter how hard the challenge. We can break down this leadership quality into two categories: *Goal perseverance* is staying the course to accomplish something difficult. *Situational perseverance* is enduring a difficult situation in life or work.

Leadership is about mobilizing groups of people to accomplish goals. Accomplishing easy things generally doesn't require much persistence. But when we set ambitious goals, they are harder to achieve, hence the need for stubborn perseverance. A leader who exhibits this kind of grit sets a positive example for team members. Goal persistence requires believing so passionately that something is possible that those around us start to believe it as well. That kind of belief and determination becomes contagious.

Situational perseverance is about facing challenging circumstances that require endurance. In the course of your working life, you will most certainly find yourself in an unending series of work situations that will require perseverance: an unhealthy work culture, deep budget cuts in your department, a promotion loss, a difficult boss, an economic downturn, an overwhelming workload, an ongoing problem with a coworker. All these situations will not only challenge your ability to endure but also test your Christian faith.

As a follower of Christ, how you respond to adversity—both as a leader and an employee—will greatly determine the effectiveness of your witness at work. If our job as Christ's ambassadors involves being "healers" of the brokenness we find in our world, then crises become some of the best opportunities we have for our witness. A Christian leader can be an "island in the storm" for people who are hurting in a difficult work environment.

If you can personally rise above the anxiety of a stressful situation with a spirit of peace, your steadiness can lift the spirits of those who are struggling. Hardship can actually provide a wonderful opportunity for you to demonstrate your faith by caring for others.

The apostle Paul's secret to persistence was to trust God to give him the strength to endure. He knew that God's purposes for his life would prevail despite his trials—perhaps even because of them. When leaders persevere in the face of adversity, they create a culture of hope—a culture that invites people to see what's possible, a culture that believes a better future is attainable. And it is hope that sustains people in the face of great adversity.

REFLECTIONS ON PERSEVERANCE

1. What most resonated with, inspired, or frustrated you in this chapter? Why?

2. Describe a time when you needed to have each type of persistence—goal and situational—and it paid off. What was the outcome? What might have happened had you not persisted?

3. Over the course of your working life, you will inevitably encounter bosses or coworkers who are extremely difficult to work with. It has often been said that people don't quit their jobs, they quit their bosses. In what ways can embodying the seventeen values of this book in your day-to-day interactions help you endure that adversity?

4. When we turn to Scripture, we see that perseverance was a core value that characterized the first-century church leaders as they faced constant trials and persecution. Both the apostles James and Paul gave us advice on how to respond in the face of persecution. Look up the following passages: Romans 12:14, 17-18; Philippians 4:12-13; and James 1:2-4. How do these passages reflect persistence? What do they mean for you as you experience work adversity?

5. Perseverance must also have limits. What are those limits in a work environment?

6. In what ways can your perseverance as a leader sustain hope and lift the spirits of your entire team in the midst of trials?

VALUE 17: LISTENING

Read chapter nineteen of *Lead Like It Matters to God*.

Key Leadership Principle: A leader who carefully and consistently listens to the people around them makes better decisions because each of those people is made in the image of God and has unique talents and insights to contribute.

Key Scripture: "The way of a fool is right in his own eyes, but a wise man listens to advice." (Proverbs 12:15 ESV)

Biologist Karl von Frisch discovered that honeybees can communicate with other members of the hive through a kind of waggle dance. This dance allows them to share information with one another about the direction and distance to water sources, to patches of flowers yielding nectar and pollen, or to a potential new nest location, and then they collaborate on their decision making. Through this repetitive "listening" process, they reach a consensus. This honeybee decision-making process models a kind of iterative democratic model for decision making that aggregates the collective wisdom of all the members of the hive.

As with honeybees, involving your team and allowing them to share their thoughts and opinions not only can result in a better decision but can create a groundswell of acceptance and good will, making the workplace "hive" happy. This comes through a commitment to listen and value the opinions of others.

The best leaders are good listeners. Good listeners benefit from hearing different opinions, gaining new insights, and getting feedback on their ideas and instincts. The more information they gather, the better the decisions they ultimately make. This is reason enough to become a good listener, but for the Christian leader, there is another profound truth about why we need to listen: the people around us are made in the image of God, each uniquely endowed with specific gifts and abilities that are different from our own. The leader who recognizes this and listens to others draws from a "divine well" and will always have an edge over a leader who does not.

When you as a leader engage a group of individuals to tackle a particular problem or decide on a specific course of action, the collective wisdom of the group—particularly one that is widely diverse—will almost always be better than your own personal instincts. At the very least, the collective wisdom will always be worth considering. This truth reinforces the Christian view of the unique giftedness of each person, as Paul described when he wrote about the collective abilities and functioning of the church as he compared us to a body (1 Corinthians 12). While a secular organization is not the same as the church, the principle holds: the people you work with are each uniquely endowed by their Creator in specific ways. Each one of them has a unique contribution, insight, and perspective to contribute to decision making.

God has surrounded us with people made in his image. When we respect them, when we listen to them, when we invite them into the grayness of a decision with us, they can help us become better leaders. And when we truly listen to others and show that we value their ideas and insights, we get another bonus—they feel affirmed and respected. Team members who feel affirmed and respected care more, work harder, and are more committed.

REFLECTIONS ON LISTENING

1. What most resonated with, inspired, or frustrated you in this chapter? Why?

2. The Bible has a quite a few pointed things to say about people who don't listen. Proverbs 12:15 is a good summary: "Fools think their own way is right, but the wise listen to advice" (NRSV). In other words, a leader who doesn't listen is a fool. Describe a time you followed a leader who didn't listen to others. What lesson did you learn from that experience?

3. Have you ever seen the slogan, "Often wrong but never in doubt"? It is an apt description of a leader who does not seek counsel. What are some ways that you as a leader can avoid the trap of ego-related overconfidence?

4. What has kept you from listening to coworkers or team members in the past?

5. In *The Wisdom of Crowds,* James Surowiecki wrote, "The powerful truth is that . . . under the right circumstances, groups are

remarkably intelligent, and are often smarter than the smartest people in them." In what ways have you found that to be true?

PUT THESE VALUES INTO PRACTICE

1. When you're forced to endure work adversity, whether goal persistence or situational persistence, try these tips: Stay positive. Do your best to embody the seventeen values in your day-to-day interactions. Be helpful and keep your eye on the greater good. Remember that ultimately you can control only your behavior, not theirs. But be patient, believing your good behavior will make a positive difference.

2. C. S. Lewis once said, "There are no ordinary people. You have never talked to a mere mortal." How might this perspective change your willingness to listen to people's opinions and thoughts—even those that don't seem "important"? Make a list of some of your team members and colleagues. For each one, identify a unique gift, talent, or perspective that you feel they can contribute to your decision making.

3. Think of a decision you are facing in your workplace that is not black and white. Rather than trying to make it on your own, seek out the insight of others on your team—not just your boss or others at the same title level as you but your whole team. Make it a practice to ask for their opinions, then listen with the goal of learning and respecting.

CONCLUSION

TAKING GOD TO WORK

Read chapter twenty of *Lead Like It Matters to God*.

Key Leadership Principle: Success is not your goal. Faithfulness to God is your goal. For the Christian leader, faithfulness is success.

Key Scripture: "Peace be with you! As the Father has sent me, I am sending you." (John 20:21)

In *Liturgy of the Ordinary*, Tish Harrison Warren sums up exactly where we are as we finish our time together in this study: "As Christians, we wake up each morning as those who are baptized. We are united with Christ and the approval of the Father is spoken over us. We are marked from our first waking moment by an identity that is given to us by grace: an identity that is deeper and more real than any identity we will don that day."

We've looked at seventeen character traits that are essential for you to embrace and live out if you want to be a "successful" leader—one who acts as God's ambassador, who handles well the "one job," the higher purpose we've been called to: to know God, to love God, and to serve God in this life.

Hopefully by this point, you are starting to see the results of seriously seeking to become a better leader, a Christian leader, a leader after God's own heart. You now have greater clarity about how your faith should play itself out at work.

I began *Lead Like It Matters to God* with the Scripture verse that totally changed my perspective on my work and my calling: "We are therefore Christ's ambassadors, as though God were making his appeal through us" (2 Corinthians 5:20). Once we grasp this astounding truth that God has anointed us to be his ambassadors and has sent us into the world with that title and responsibility, it changes everything. I pray it has changed everything for you.

What a true honor God has entrusted to us! We no longer need to show up at work just to get a paycheck or seek professional accolades. We show up for a greater purpose, knowing that our workplace is exactly where God wants us to be change agents for his kingdom. Jesus has sent us into the work world: "As the Father has sent me, I am sending you." Your workplace and your community are the mission fields where you have the greatest calling to live out that ambassadorial vocation and identity.

As I have argued in this study, our light shines brightest when we embrace and display the values of Christ's coming kingdom—values like integrity, excellence, courage, love, humility, encouragement, perseverance, generosity, listening, and forgiveness—as Christ shines through us. When we do this consistently, we stand out, we set ourselves apart, and we provoke the question to which Christ is the answer. That's what our ambassador status looks like in practice.

In 2 Corinthians 2:15, Paul encourages us in our work as he reminds us that "we are to God the fragrance of Christ among those who are being saved and among those who are perishing" (NKJV). As Christ's ambassadors, we are no longer held captive by the allure of success as the world defines it. Mother Teresa made a remarkable statement, "God did not call me to be successful, he called me to be faithful." She redefined success for a follower of Christ—faithfulness is success, and success is faithfulness.

While being successful in the conventional sense of the word is not a bad thing, it's not the main thing for Christian leaders. So even though we are incarnating these seventeen qualities, we must be wary of anything that tempts us back into an old way of thinking about success. We are to work with excellence and diligence wherever we serve, not because *success* is our goal but because *faithfulness* is our goal.

One of the remarkable truths about our faith is that God has chosen to use us at all, flawed as we are. He could have chosen to intervene in our world more directly himself. But he invited us to participate in his great revolution to change the world. He has called us to be his transformed people engaged in transforming the world, making it more pleasing to him.

Rest assured, in our service to the Lord as we lead our groups, we will make mistakes, we will suffer setbacks, we will experience failures. *But* we can still trust that God is using us.

Faithful, not successful, is all he asks. If you are faithful, God will use you to accomplish great things—even when your impact seems insignificant and you don't see any positive outcomes from your witness. Even when you feel like a failure, God is working through you. And you can claim this reassuring truth: *What God is accomplishing through you involves you, but it does not depend on you.* The real harvest of your faithfulness is something you may never see, as God works in the lives of the people you interact with every day. In the words of Mother Teresa, we are all "little pencils" in the hand of a writing God who is sending a love letter to the world.

REFLECTIONS TO CONSIDER

1. Now that you've gone through *Lead Like It Matters to God*, what changes do you want to make in your leadership?

2. In what ways have you redefined the idea of success?

3. Which of these seventeen leadership qualities do you struggle with the most? Why? What could help you embrace them?

4. Have you ever struggled with believing that God wants faithfulness, not success? Or that he can't use you because you make mistakes and are flawed? What can you do when you experience those feelings to remind yourself that God accepts you and wants to use you?

5. Think of a leader you respect who has been faithful. What has most impressed you about the way that leader conducts himself or herself?

6. When you reach the end of your working career, what would be the most meaningful compliments that you would hope to hear at your retirement party? Would you want them to be about your accomplishments or your character? Explain.